Dreams in Stone   The University of Chicago

Dreams in Stone   The University of Chicago

International Standard Book Number: 0-917804
Library of Congress Catalog Card Number: 76-44578
Printed in the United States of America

Published by The Vice-President for Public Affairs, The University of Chicago
Photographs by Patrice Grimbert and Jose Lopez and Luis Medina
Editors: D. J. R. Bruckner and Irene Macauley
Design: Ray Machura
Printed by the R.R.Donnelley & Sons Company

Contents

Introduction   vii

The Pictures   3

Index to Buildings   272

Index to Architects   274

The University of Chicago
Campus Map   277

These Mansions of the Mind

On June 25, 1891, Henry Ives Cobb presented to the Trustees of the new University of Chicago a drawing of his plan for the University. Thomas W. Goodspeed said it seemed then "a dream of a far distant future." But, he added, only 25 years "saw the dream practically transmuted into enduring stone."* It is blue Bedford stone. Goodspeed wrote at a time when all the buildings were Gothic. Many more enduring stones, and other durable materials, have shaped many dreams in other styles since his time; but Cobb's plan, for a university built in quadrangles, still dominates and it governs the minds of the later dreamers.

Two new buildings were built while the pictures in this book were being made: the Surgery-Brain Research Pavilion and the Marjorie Kovler Viral Oncology Laboratory. They are not in the book. One has to stop at some time, though the University changes all the time. So many dreams, so many stones. There is constant addition, renovation, repair. In this book you will find pictures of 125 buildings on the Midway campus and of Yerkes Observatory in Wisconsin: the University as it was in the winter of 1973-74 when I commissioned the pictures.

"We are the pioneers of an immeasurable future," John Henry Barrows, a Chicago pastor and University booster, said at the dedication of Haskell Hall in 1893, referring to "this work of University building that shall make our city beautiful and illustrious to the ends of the earth and the limits of time." Public speech was grand in those days. Nonetheless, it is obvious that the builders wanted the University to appear lovely, enchanting, even seductive. The first builders of the place—Trustees, donors, and faculty—said Goodspeed, "believed in the cultural influence of architecture." He added that it was their hope for the University "that the passing of years among its beautiful structures might increase intelligence, refine taste, and develop character, and thus minister to the highest culture."

In the beginning of their deliberations, the Trustees had decided the style of the University would be English Gothic. The members of the Trustees' committee on the buildings, and Cobb, in their correspondence made it clear they were thinking primarily of Oxford. There was an earlier time when that place and its style was not so respected, of course, not even in England. One thinks of the pleasant irony William Hazlitt wrote in the *London Magazine* in 1823 describing the Oxford buildings as "the monuments and lordly mansions of the mind of man" and declaring that "we could pass our lives in Oxford without having or wanting any other idea—that of the place is enough." Two generations later his smile would have scandalized everyone, including the boisterously democratic Chicagoans.

The time of the first building at Chicago, William Gardner Hale later recalled, was "a time of great mental exaltation. The World's Fair was in the making." Indeed, the fair of 1893 was being made just across the Midway. Its fantastic temporary wooden and plaster buildings were painted white and its promoters publicized it throughout the world as the White City. It was

*A History of the University of Chicago 1891-1916. University of Chicago Press. 1916. P. 172.

Hale who, in 1893, began calling the new University next door "the Grey City of enduring stone," and the name became enshrined in the "Alma Mater." But even the name is owing to Oxford. Goodspeed reminds us that William Morris, in a famous book published in 1883, wrote that "there are many places in England where a young man may get as good book learning as in Oxford: not one where he can receive the education which the loveliness of the gray city used to give." Hermann Zapf, that great alphabet-maker and artist of our time, says a little reflection on Morris will make you realize what a "spell" Gothic had cast on the western world in those days. His word is a good one. Oxford is not grey at all; it is mostly built of Portland stone which is yellow. But the notion of a grey city was a strong one, once the formula was pronounced, and the blue Bedford stone of Chicago does indeed look grey; but it is my guess that the Chicagoans, filled with what the Rev. Mr. Barrow called "the natural desire for a splendid earthly immortality," would have called the University "the grey city" if it had been made of red brick or white wood. They wanted that connection. In a sense, they made it, too. Chicago will make any old Oxonian somewhat nostalgic in spite of himself, not by imitation, for there is little of it, but in feeling, by sensible hints. Presumably that is what Goodspeed meant by cultural influence; just so, there comes to one in Oxford itself a kind of essential nostalgia for a time and country that have always been lost to all mankind.

In any case, the builders, from the beginning, cared about what they built. It was the golden age of the Chicago School of architecture, and the Gothic style was certainly not the newest thing, but, through the years, the best firms and many of the best architects in the city and the nation came to build here. The standard has stayed high; indeed, the names of the architects who have built here in the last 30 years may be more enduring than those of the earlier decades and the new buildings include some of the best in the modern world. Presumably, if architecture still exerts a cultural influence, the member of the University today falls mostly under the spell of the massive and yet graceful Joseph Regenstein Library much more than under that of towers, turrets and gargoyles. But the spirit of the place is Cobb's plan, which gives it its peculiar character. It would be wonderful in any case to find a campus so large, of such tranquillity and grandeur, in the midst of a tremendous modern city; to find this one, in Chicago, is simply stunning. The original style was out of fashion for a long time, of course, and the craftsmen skilled in it are no more, but the central part of the campus is one of the largest projects of architectural preservation in the country and it is interesting to find the critics once again calling the campus "the cultural mile." Goodspeed would be delighted to hear it.

Besides, whatever the taste, Gothic can be entertaining, whether the buildings were put up in the days of great Gothic builders or, as in the case of the University, long afterwards. Among western styles, the characteristic mark of Gothic is that it is so often funny. It makes you smile, especially in its decoration.

There are styles more awesome, most seem to me more noble; but in Gothic it is clear the builders had fun. I have looked at some of the drawings by Cobb and other architects who worked on the University. My feeling is right: there are finials, decorations, gargoyles, faces, drawn freehand on the sketches, unfinished most often, but grinning, fantastic, dreamy. That is a good sign. Cultural influences should be delightful.

The Pictures

Cartier-Bresson talked about "the precise moment" of a photograph. I suppose the moment of this book was the time I made a contract with a photographer to begin the pictures, at the end of 1973. Later, a team of two photographers finished the project. The entire undertaking took about two years. Almost 2,000 photographs were taken, of which I selected about 1,000 for printing; from these the pictures in the book were chosen. My direction to the photographers was to make pictures of each building. So, on the whole, the pictures do not include people and, if there is a sense of movement, it is the movement of the eye of the architect and the hand of the builder. The entire archive of pictures was made for that purpose, and it was made new; this collection is not historical.

The photographs and the pictures in the book are quite different objects, of course. And the photographs themselves are more than representations of the buildings. Their eternity is their own, a unique moment. The pictures will survive some of the subjects:

rooms will be remodeled, stairwells closed, windows replaced. The light will never be the same in any eye, nor on any paper. For many, the pictures will be the memory, in place of the memory of the place itself; "time out of mind" is the right phrase here. The picture you see is not an illusion; your memory of the building in the photograph is one.

When the pictures were commissioned and when I decided to make a book from them, I wanted people to see, remember or imagine the University. It is not a "scenic" book, however, nor in any sense a complete guide. Many familiar "views" are not in it; indeed, the point of view in any one picture is not yours, you will find. It never is. But it is the photograph as an object that reminds you of that. To me the greatest difference between looking at the pictures and looking at the buildings is that time is of no importance in the pictures, but the buildings, looked at, suggest time passing, their own history, movement and action. The message of the photographs is their own, not the imagination's.

The Photographers

Three photographers made the pictures from which those in this book were selected: Patrice Grimbert, and Luis Medina and Jose Lopez. Grimbert's photographs are noted by the initials "PG" below his pictures. All the others in the book are by Medina and Lopez who work as a team and who refer to themselves professionally as Lopez-Medina. I have never met anyone who could tell which of them took any picture they exhibit.

Patrice Grimbert. The face you see here in the picture, in front of Ida Noyes Hall, is Patrice Grimbert's. He described it as "the photographer making a mistake." It is a happy mistake. It is our only picture of him, and he is dead. In 1973, when he began photographing the University, he was in the MFA program at the School of the Art Institute of Chicago, and was teaching at a suburban school and at Columbia College. His wife, Joan, was a graduate student at the University. Patrice had printed the photographs of a friend of his who had died—Richard Nickel—for an Art Institute show, and had made his own collection of pictures of Chicago buildings, pictures of extraordinary power.

He was born in France in 1947. In 1962 he began to work for Air France and, in the next seven years, as he travelled in 40 countries, he made a collection of more than 10,000 photographs and slides. In 1969, he was one of 12 photographers chosen to study in the Stage Experimental Photographique which Jean-Pierre Sudre created in Paris. It was during this year that Patrice mastered the darkroom technique which was so special with him. After the year at SEP, he and a colleague worked as photographers and printers of photographs, for the Rheims & Laurin auction house, on many special exhibits, and as printers for other photographers. His wife, whom he married in Paris, is an American. In 1971 they decided to move from Paris to Chicago.

Patrice and I first discussed the University's pictures late in 1973. Our contract specified that he would make not less than 1,000 photographs in two years. Not many men would not be intimidated by such an order, but Patrice had the good humor of a man who takes seriously what he does. For a few days he and I walked through the University together, climbing up into towers and across roofs, opening doors we had never seen into strange rooms, all the time discussing what pictures might be made. Since I had never been a student here and was new to the place, the discovery was mine and his at the same time and he is bound up in my memory of the place forever. He then outlined on a calendar the work he was committed to. He had a rare sense of order and of the power good work has to inspire in a man. His wife says he told her on April 16 that he had taken 17 photographs that day and would take 18 the next; it sounds like him.

On April 17, he awakened with a debilitating headache and was taken to the University's hospital where he sank into a coma and died, of a cerebral hemorrhage, on April 19. He was 27. He had made about 100 photographs of the University.

Patrice had exhibited in the 1972 Gamma 1 Exhibition (Chicago Photo One). His work is included in collections in the Art Institute of Chicago, the Bibliothèque Nationale (Paris), and in a number of private collections.

Lopez-Medina. In June 1974, Lopez and Medina, who knew Patrice and his work, agreed to complete the archive of the pictures of the University. In effect, this meant they had to agree to photograph the entire place, treating Patrice's pictures as a separate collection, and they agreed to the same contractual terms.

They were older than Patrice and had been professional photographers longer, with a number of important shows to their credit and a good deal of critical acclaim to recommend them. They had work in hand and work committed at the time I asked them to photograph the University. They completed this enormous labor in the time agreed on, making not a mere thousand photographs, but many hundreds more and printing every one I ordered. They could have made a better living easily, and with greater comfort to themselves; what they did here is as astonishing in its generosity as in the beauty and power of the photographs.

They had known the University longer than I did. They had much experience in making architectural pictures. They had to work with someone, me, who had little knowledge of photography and a brief acquaintance with the buildings, but who had to choose the pictures to be printed. They printed what was ordered, but never changed their own judgments about what was best in their own work. Lavater once said you should not pretend to know a man until you have divided an estate with him. The estate I divided with them was theirs; so, we know one another. Their candor, decency and good humor were as important throughout this project as was any art.

Jose was born in 1941 and Luis in 1942, both in Havana; they grew up and were educated together, and both left Cuba in 1959. When they came to Chicago in 1966, they entered the Art Institute School as majors in sculpture, but soon changed their interests to photography. In 1971, working with funds from the award of the

Fred J. Forster Travelling Fellowship which the Art Institute gives to a graduating student, they made a collection of pictures of Chicago buildings and people. The work, and especially their two-man show at the Institute in 1973, made them celebrated. Their work has been shown in 18 galleries in this country and abroad in five years, and is represented in the permanent collections of the Art Institute of Chicago, the Boston Museum of Fine Arts, the Addison Gallery of American Art in Andover, the National Gallery of Victoria in Melbourne, the University of Chicago, the University of Minnesota, the Quincy Society of Fine Arts, the Seagram Collection, and many others.

The True Begetters
Irene Macauley, the Director of Publications in the Office of Public Affairs at the University, made the entire project happen. She scheduled the work and logged it; she was, first, the liaison with the photographers and, then, the overall director of their work; she even found an ingenious carpenter to make the oak cases for the photographs. She arranged access, security, the ordering of special equipment; and she kept all the accounts. At those too frequent moments when exhaustion made everyone else indifferent, she shamed us all back into orderly work by demonstrating, without saying, that she thoroughly and completely loved the whole project. If anyone really made this book, she did it, often by making the rest of us do things we did not know how to do and probably could not do again without her.

Ray Machura, of R. R. Donnelley & Sons Co., designed the book. The complexity and size of the task are obvious. What those of us who worked with him will not forget, and what is not obvious, is his tactful personal strength, a hard determination and clear judgment that never failed even when Irene and I and the photographers would all take quite different positions and the production people at Donnelley's would suggest delicately that perhaps what any or all of us wanted might be technically impossible. Ray made it possible.

In a real sense, the initiators of the photographing were Leslie and David Travis. When I began to discuss a picture book in 1973, Leslie, who had grown up in Hyde Park and was teaching in local schools, was also a freelance photographer who took pictures occasionally for the University's Office of Public Information. David, her husband, is the photographic curator for the Art Institute. It was Leslie who first came and talked to me about Patrice Grimbert. She never left her own values in doubt. "He is a great photographer," she said, "and you have the chance, if you can get him, to have his first major collection of pictures." She was right. After Patrice died, I called Leslie one day and asked her to stop by. She came up to my office and told me I should talk with Luis and Jose, and she offered to talk with them herself. She then expressed perfectly the pain of that time and the power of the emotions of all of us. She said: "I want to see this book succeed. Otherwise, I would never have come up here now." That desire to see good and difficult things succeed is the special gift of the

Travises. They have kept an interest in every detail of this long project. When we have called them, they have come to help, at our convenience. There may have been a book and a collection of pictures without them, but not this one. They gave endlessly the best they have: their appreciation, encouragement, judgment, their affectionate knowledge of a world of art.

To Joan Grimbert one can only express gratitude. There is no way to know how great was the cost to her of collecting, identifying and dating, and turning over to us the pictures Patrice left in his darkroom when he died. She took a hand in developing some and made sure the rest were properly printed. In a time when it seems incredible that she could have done it, she justified his written schedules, showing us what he had done and what was to be done, reconciled all the accounts, and comforted us for her loss.

William M. Murphy, a graduate student in history at the University, who had collaborated with me on that collection of presidential papers, *The Idea of the University of Chicago*, researched the archives for dates and identifications of buildings, donors, architects, decorations, the many remodellings; and he exposed to us the many lacunae in the records.

It was Edward Levi, when he was president of the University, who started the entire affair by saying one day that "we need a picture book, a book of the buildings, without too much text." I intend not to ask him whether this is what he had in mind. John Wilson, both when he was Provost and as President, steadily encouraged us with questions, suggestions, and a lot of the more

costly support which was not easily found in those years. He even took long hours to go through the photographs with us as we built the archive; and, in that gentle way he has, when will power had failed us entirely, he would revive it by asking suddenly exactly *when* he could expect to see the book. Such a question from such a man has to have an answer, after all, and a positive one.

There are many others who contributed in many ways to this work. There are scores whose names I did not record—architects, artists, photographers and critics, journalists and scholars from a number of countries. There are more than 60 names in my file of notes about people who consulted or suggested. Perhaps it is enough to say that special thanks are due to people in the Office of Public Information, especially to Eva Maddox, who helped log and research; to the Special Events Office, the Plant Department and to Buildings & Grounds personnel and the Security people at the University, to the University Architect and his associates, to a number of editors and the Director of the University Press for their interest and advice, and to a group of splendid craftsmen at the Donnelley Company.

A Little Guide To A Big Book
The text of the captions with the pictures is limited to the names of the buildings or the locations of particular parts of the buildings, identification of the architects, the dates of construction and renovation, and, in a few cases, captious remarks by me.

The information is incomplete in several ways. The dates are not uniform. Some refer to the dates of the plans for the buildings, if we know them; others refer to the dates of the beginning of construction if that is all we know.

Renovation is noted only where it has resulted in significant changes in the structures inside or outside.

The sequence of pictures was determined by my walking habits. I thought about how I usually take people on a walk around the campus, and then narrated my habit to Irene Macauley who, using a map overlay, divided the campus into sections. Together, we then decided how we would begin a tour of buildings within each section and where we would enter the next section.

At the back is a map which you can fold out for reference as you look at the pictures. It is a mosaic made from aerial photographs of the campus, cut up and assembled by Donnelley's map makers under the supervision of Duncan Fitchet. The University can not be seen this way, of course; the map is an illusion, but a lovely one and a fine guide.

At the back also there are two indexes, one of buildings and one of architects.

The entire archive of photographs, printed by the photographers, along with the proofs and the negatives and all the records of the project, have been made part of the University's permanent collections.

D. J. R. BRUCKNER
August 1976

William Rainey Harper Memorial Library
William Wieboldt Hall
Business East
Julius Rosenwald Hall
George C. Walker Museum
Albert Pick Hall for International Studies
Women's Quadrangle
Jerome Beecher Hall
Turpin and Martha Green Hall
E. G. Kelly Hall
Nancy Foster Hall
Social Science Research Building

Overleaf: William Rainey Harper Memorial Library.
Shepley, Rutan & Coolidge, 1912.
West tower, south elevation.

William Rainey Harper Memorial Library.

Architects: Shepley, Rutan & Coolidge, 1912.

Renovation of interior by Metz, Train, Olson & Youngren, Inc., 1973.

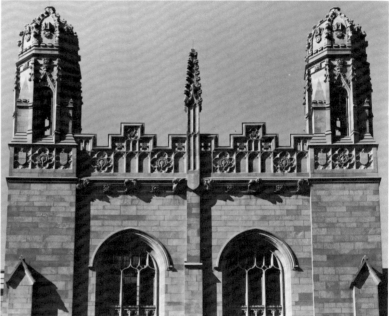

Harper from the Midway. Linné monument in foreground.

West Tower, symbolizing the Church.

West Tower—south front. Arms of the universities of London, Leyden, Göttingen, Uppsala, Aberdeen, Brussels, Paris, Berlin, Salamanca, Leipzig, Heidelberg, Geneva, Manchester, and Vienna.

Harper: Center door from Harper Court.

West door from Harper Court.

Room 284.

Harper Library Main Reading Room, looking west.

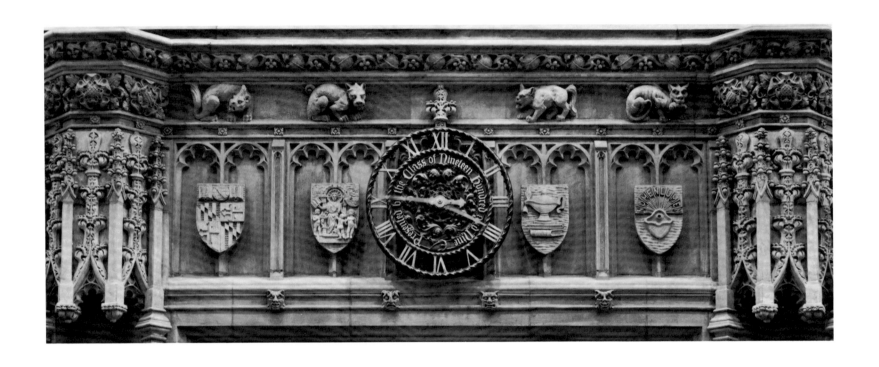

Reading Room—screen over the west entrance, with arms of Johns Hopkins,
Columbia, Michigan, and Wisconsin universities.

9

Harper: Reading Room ceiling.
Corbel supporting arch.

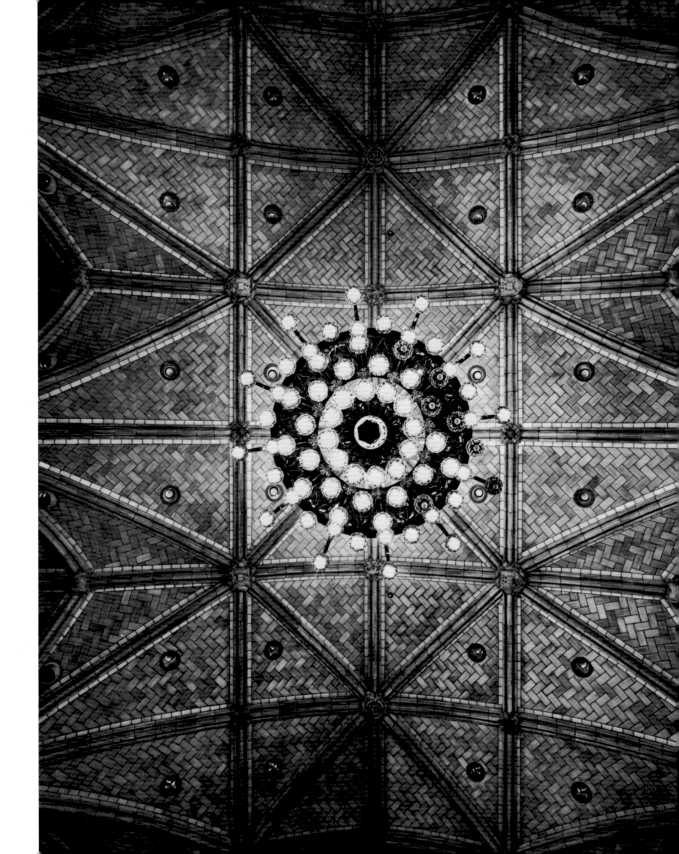

The ceiling—from below.

William Wieboldt Hall.

Architects: Coolidge & Hodgdon, 1926.

Renovation of interiors by Metz, Train, Olson & Youngren, Inc., 1973.

Classics Building left of tower.

Entrance from the Midway.

Wieboldt: Detail over Midway arch.

Detail from archway entrance.

Corbel supporting arch.

Business East.

Architects: Shepley, Rutan & Coolidge, 1904.

Renovation by Samuel A. Lichtmann and Metz, Train, Olson & Youngren, Inc., 1974.

Originally, the Law School.

Rosenwald Hall (1914), Business East (1904), and bridge (1972).   Business East: West door from Harper Court.

Bridge to Harper Library.

Business East entrance.

Stairwell at first floor.
First-floor stairway.

Third-floor reading room, now part of the College Library.

Julius Rosenwald Hall.

Architects: Holabird & Roche, 1914.

Renovation by Samuel A. Lichtmann and Metz, Train, Olson & Youngren, Inc., 1972.

West elevation.

South door and octagonal Tower of the Winds.

Rosenwald: Octagonal tower from the west.

First-floor office.

Top of tower stairwell.

Faculty Lounge.

George C. Walker Museum.
Architect: Henry Ives Cobb, 1893.
South facade of tower.

Tower stairwell.

Albert Pick Hall for International Studies.
Architects: Ralph Rapson and Associates, Burnham and Hammond, J. Lee Jones, 1971.
East front.

Second-floor office.

Women's Quadrangle, looking north—University barometer in foreground.

Jerome Beecher Hall, Turpin and Martha Green Hall, and E. G. Kelly Hall.
Architect: Henry Ives Cobb (Beecher and Kelly, 1893; Green, 1899).

Nancy Foster Hall.

Architect: Henry Ives Cobb, 1893.

Social Science Research Building.

Architects: Coolidge & Hodgdon, 1929.

The south bay.

Social Science: Room 122, lecture hall.

Classics Building : Hiram Kelly Memorial
Thomas Wakefield Goodspeed Hall
Frederick T. Gates Hall
E. Nelson Blake Hall
Silas B. Cobb Lecture Hall
Swift Hall
Joseph Bond Chapel
Frederick Haskell Hall
Administration Building
University Bookstore
Ingleside Hall

Overleaf: Frederick T. Gates Hall.
Henry Ives Cobb, 1892.
East elevation.

Classics Building:
Hiram Kelly Memorial.

Architects: Shepley, Rutan & Coolidge, 1914.
North door.

Classics staircase to second floor.

Detail from staircase.

Classics: Third-floor Reading Room.

Reading Room ceiling.
The arms of Erasmus, carved in oak.

Thomas Wakefield Goodspeed Hall, Frederick T. Gates Hall, and E. Nelson Blake Hall.
Architect: Henry Ives Cobb, 1892.

Blake Hall (left) from Graduate Quadrangle.

Silas B. Cobb Lecture Hall.

Architect: Henry Ives Cobb, 1892.

Renovation by Burnham & Hammond, 1968.

Central tower.

41

Swift Hall.

Architects: Coolidge & Hodgdon, 1926.

From northwest.

Cloister, west wall, and stone garden.

Cloister entrance.

Ceiling detail.

Swift: First floor, west corridor.

The Common Room.

Divine messenger in the Reading Room ceiling.

Third-floor Reading Room.

The Dean's Office.

Joseph Bond Chapel.

Architects: Coolidge & Hodgdon, 1926.

Left: East facade.

Above: South elevation.

Bond: West window. In the tablet below, John VIII: 32.

Adam in the west wall.

PG

PG

The east window.

East door.

Bond Chapel interior.

The west window.

Bond interior: North wall and window.

Dove in east window.
Chancel.

Bronze plaque by Lorado Taft.
Angel at the foot of the ceiling.
The altar.

Frederick Haskell Hall.

Architect: Henry Ives Cobb, 1896.

Originally Haskell Oriental Museum.

Left: Facing Harper Court.

First-floor staircase.

Administration Building.

Architects: Holabird, Root & Burgee, 1948.

University Bookstore.

Architects: Shepley, Rutan & Coolidge, 1902.

Originally the University Press Building.

Printing Department, fourth floor.

Ingleside Hall.
Architect: C. B. Atwood, 1897.   South bay.

(Sidney A.) Kent Chemical Laboratory
George Herbert Jones Laboratory
Searle Chemistry Laboratory
Snell Hall
Charles Hitchcock Hall
Anatomy Building
Helen Culver Hall

Overleaf: George Herbert Jones Laboratory.

Coolidge & Hodgdon, 1929.

South elevation.

(Sidney A.) Kent Chemical Laboratory.

Architect: Henry Ives Cobb, 1894.

Kent: Gable ornament.

The south door.

Lecture Theater.

The Lecture Theater interior.

Theater ceiling.

George Herbert Jones Laboratory.
Architects: Coolidge & Hodgdon, 1929.

Panes in east door.

East entrance from the Main Quadrangle.

Vestibule with bust of George Herbert Jones.

Searle Chemistry Laboratory.

Architects: Smith, Smith, Haines, Lundberg & Waehler, 1968.

West facade.

Snell Hall.

Architect: Henry Ives Cobb, 1893.

Charles Hitchcock Hall.

Architect: Dwight H. Perkins, 1902.

Renovation of interior by Hausner & Macsai and by John Macsai Associates, 1970-73.

North side.

Southeast bay and tower.

Hitchcock: Midwestern flora around the door.

South door.

A room in the resident master's suite.

Anatomy Building.

Architect: Henry Ives Cobb, 1897.

North side.

Anatomy: Griffon supporting eave.

North face, looking east.

Helen Culver Hall.

Architect: Henry Ives Cobb, 1897.

West side.

Culver Hall: Southwest corner.

(Martin A.) Ryerson Physical Laboratory
Bernard Albert Eckhart Hall
Leon Mandel Assembly Hall
Joseph Reynolds Student Clubhouse
John J. Mitchell Tower
Charles L. Hutchinson Hall
Zoology Building
Ida B. and Walter Erman Biology Center

Overleaf: Leon Mandel Assembly Hall.

Shepley, Rutan & Coolidge, 1901.

Section through Assembly Hall.

(Martin A.) Ryerson Physical Laboratory.

Architect: Henry Ives Cobb, 1893. Annex by Shepley, Rutan & Coolidge, 1910.

South front, facing Main Quadrangle.

Ryerson: West gable and tower.

Front door from the Quadrangle.   Tower staircases.

Bernard Albert Eckhart Hall.

Architect: Charles Z. Klauder, 1929.

South front, on the Main Quadrangle.

Bridge from Ryerson to Eckhart.

Doors to second-floor Common Room.

The Common Room.

Leon Mandel Assembly Hall.
Architects: Shepley, Rutan & Coolidge, 1901.
East elevation on University Avenue.

The east entrance.

Vent windows, gargoyles, crenelles, and the curly lion—north side.

PG

Mandel Hall: West side from Hutchinson Commons.

West door from Hutchinson Court.

Mandel interior: The stage from the balcony with window covers drawn closed.

PG

Face at base of proscenium arch.

West balcony and windows—the window to the right was made by Louis Tiffany, for the class of 1902.

Mandel: Ceilings and lights in entrance foyer.

Hallway from the balcony.

The auditorium from the stage.

Joseph Reynolds Student Clubhouse.

Architects: Shepley, Rutan & Coolidge, 1901.

Lobby from the main stairwell.

The north lounge.

Main stairwell from first floor.

Reynolds Club south lounge seen through Mandel corridor window.

Reynolds: East side, from University Avenue and 57th Street.

John J. Mitchell Tower.

Architects: Shepley, Rutan & Coolidge, 1901.

West face in sunlight, with moon.

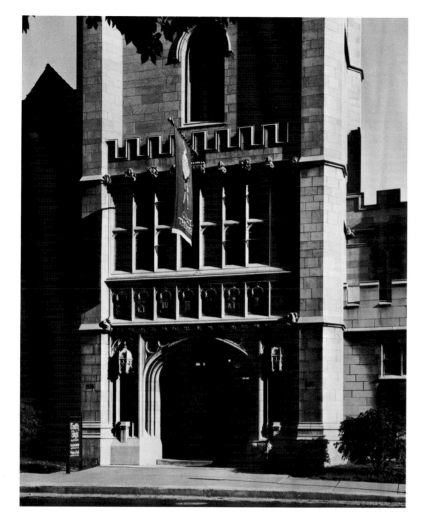

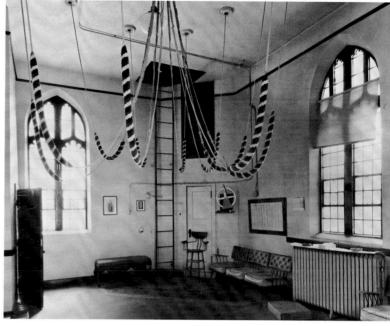

Mitchell Tower: North door on 57th Street.

Ringing room under the Mitchell Tower belfry.

The University Seal in the floor under the Tower, gift of the class of 1911.

Arches and gallery windows in Tower entrance.

Stairs from Tower foyer into Hutchinson Hall.

Mitchell Tower: Little lounge in Tower foyer.

"Joyfully to recall Alice Freeman Palmer, Dean of Women in the University, 1892-1895, these bells make music."

PG

Charles L. Hutchinson Hall.

Architects: Shepley, Rutan & Coolidge, 1901.

South side, from Hutchinson Court.

PG

Hutchinson Hall: South side looking west from Reynolds Club.

North side and west face from 57th Street.

Hutchinson Commons interior, from balcony over east door.

Hammer-beam ceiling.

Faces under the balcony.

Fireplace in south wall.

Zoology Building.

Architect: Henry Ives Cobb, 1897.

North facade on 57th Street.

North face.

South face from Botany Pond.

PG

Left to right: Culver, Anatomy, Zoology, and Biology—the Hull Biological
Laboratories—which surround Hull Court.

Ida B. and Walter Erman Biology Center.

Architect: Henry Ives Cobb, 1897.

West side, through Hull Gate. Originally Botany Building.

Erman: From Hutchinson Court.

East door.

Hull Court
Hull Gate
Cobb Gate
Joseph Regenstein Library
"Nuclear Energy"
Frank Dickinson Bartlett Gymnasium

Overleaf: Frank Dickinson Bartlett Gymnasium.
Shepley, Rutan & Coolidge, 1904.
East elevation.

Hull Court: South entrance—Hull Gate.
Botany Pond, in foreground.
Designed by Olmstead Brothers, 1903.

Hull Gate.

Iron, stone, and glass.

PG

Hull Court: Looking west toward Culver and Anatomy.

Cobb Gate.

Architect: Henry Ives Cobb, 1900.

From inside Hull Court.

Cobb Gate: Fourth-year student triumphant.
Admissions officer defying entrant.

The gates in Cobb Gate.

Cobb Gate from 57th Street.

From Regenstein Library.

The Joseph Regenstein Library.

Architects: Skidmore, Owings & Merrill—Walter Netsch, senior architect—1967.

From the southeast.

Looking north and east from roof of Hinds Laboratory.

Regenstein: South face.

"Nuclear Energy" by Henry Moore, 1967.

Right: North face of central section.

118

Regenstein: Special Collections.   View from first floor looking north.

Grand staircase between second and third floors.

Regenstein: Natural movement up stairs.

Stairs afloat.

Frank Dickinson Bartlett Gymnasium.

Architects: Shepley, Rutan & Coolidge, 1904.

West facade, from Regenstein Library steps.

Bartlett: West tower.

East entrance on University Avenue.

East entrance foyer and stairs.

Bartlett: Window in east stairwell,
"The crowning of Ivanhoe by Rowena,"
designed by Edward D. S. Perry, 1904.

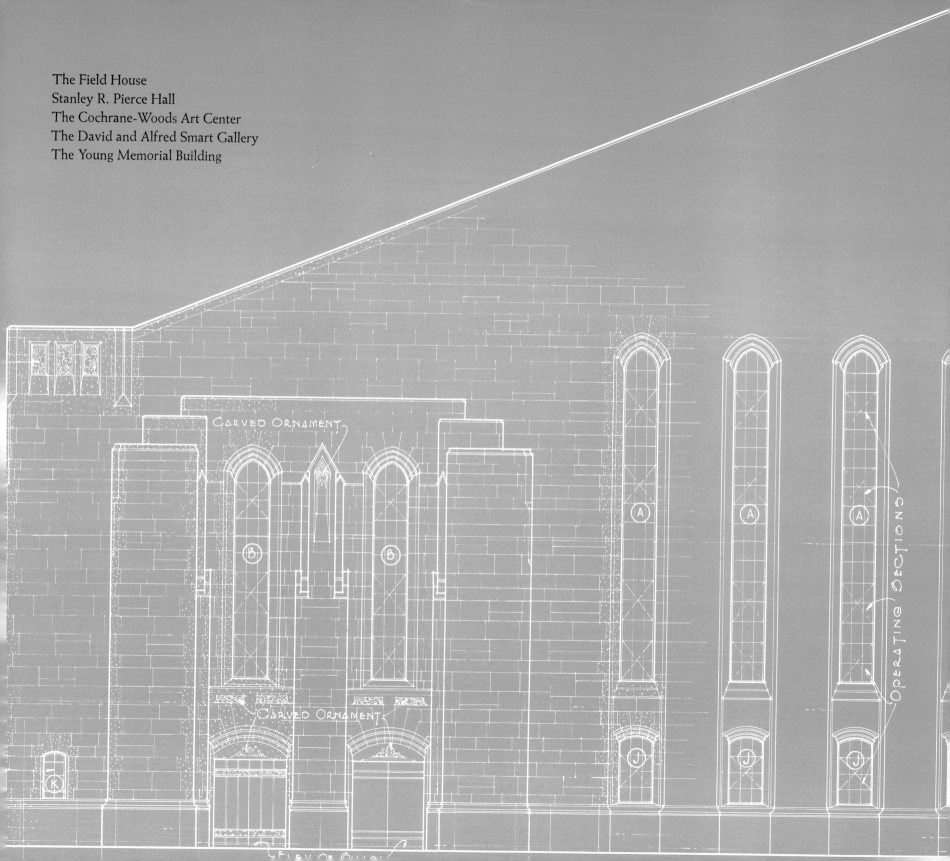

The Field House
Stanley R. Pierce Hall
The Cochrane-Woods Art Center
The David and Alfred Smart Gallery
The Young Memorial Building

Overleaf: The Field House.
Holabird & Root, 1931.
East elevation.

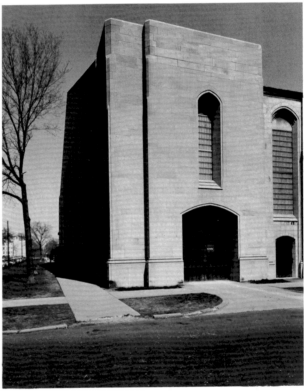

The Field House.

Architects: Holabird & Root, 1931.

Looking northeast from Regenstein Library.

East entrance.

129

Stanley R. Pierce Hall.
Architects: Harry Weese and Associates, 1960.
Student residence.

The Cochrane-Woods Art Center.
Architect: Edward Larabee Barnes, 1971.
East entrance.

Cochrane-Woods Art Center: North side from the courtyard.

The David and Alfred Smart Gallery.

Architect: Edward Larabee Barnes, 1974.

Opening day.

The Gallery's main hall.

The Young Memorial Building.

Architect unknown. Erected about 1898.

Originally part of the Chicago Home for Incurables,
now the home of the University Architect, Housing, and Security.

Research Institutes
Enrico Fermi Institute
James Franck Institute
Accelerator Building
Computer Building
High Energy Physics Building
Laboratory for Astrophysics and Space Research
Charles Reid Barnes Laboratory
Botany Greenhouses

Overleaf: Charles Reid Barnes Laboratory.

Perkins, Chatten & Hammond, 1930.

East elevation.

Research Institutes—Enrico Fermi Institute and James Franck Institute—
and Accelerator Building.

Architects: Schmidt, Garden & Erikson (Research Institutes, 1950; Accelerator Building, 1951).

East side—on Ellis Avenue, 56th to 57th Street.

In the Accelerator Building: Space satellite in the making.

Computer Building.
Architects: Schmidt, Garden & Erikson, 1971.
Research Institutes in background.

High Energy Physics Building.
Architects: Hausner and Macsai, 1967.
South side.

Laboratory for Astrophysics and Space Research.
Architects: Skidmore, Owings & Merrill, 1964.
South front.

East wall, looking north.

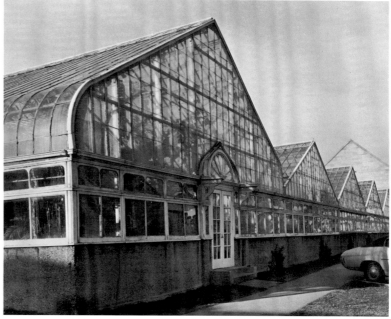

Charles Reid Barnes Laboratory and Botany Greenhouses.
Architects: Perkins, Chatten & Hammond, 1930.

Greenhouse door under sunrise window.

The Greenhouses.

Charles O. Whitman Laboratory for Experimental Zoology
Experimental Biology
Henry Hinds Laboratory for the Geophysical Sciences
Zoller Research Facility
Cummings Life Science Center
Dallas B. Phemister Hall

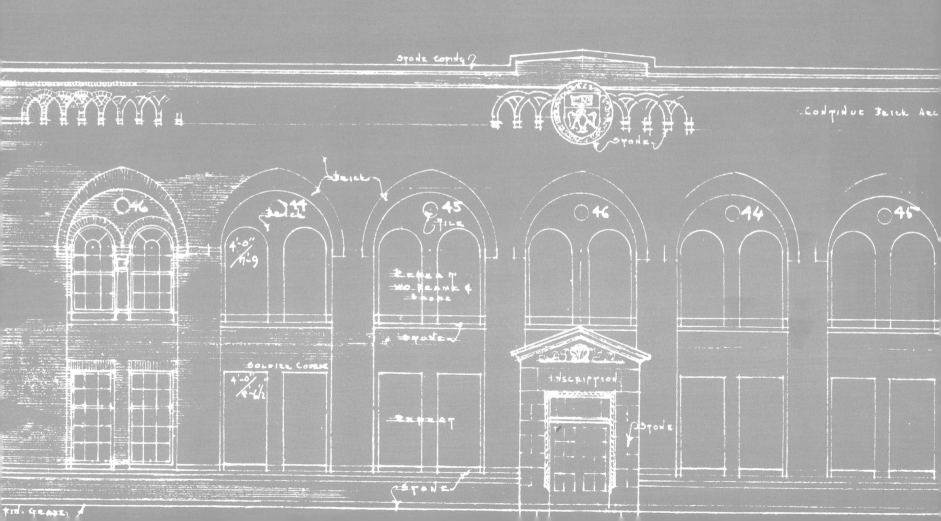

Overleaf: Charles O. Whitman Laboratory for Experimental Zoology.

Coolidge & Hodgdon, 1929.

North elevation.

Charles O. Whitman Laboratory for Experimental Zoology.

Architects: Coolidge & Hodgdon, 1926.

Whitman's rooster.   Whitman's phoenix.

Experimental Biology.
Architects: Burnham & Hammond, 1949.
Originally the American Meat Institute.

Henry Hinds Laboratory for the Geophysical Sciences.
Architect: J. W. Colburn, 1969.
East front and entrance.

Front entrance brickwork.

In the entryway: "Earth, Water, Sky," ceramic by Ruth Duckworth, 1969.

Ceiling from below.

West wall of entryway.

Zoller Research Facility.

No architect, 1941.

Well, every place has to have *one....*

Cummings Life Science Center.

Architects: J. W. Colburn & Associates and Schmidt, Garden & Erikson, 1970.

Looking west from Hinds roof.

Dallas B. Phemister Hall.

Architect: Eero Saarinen, 1958.

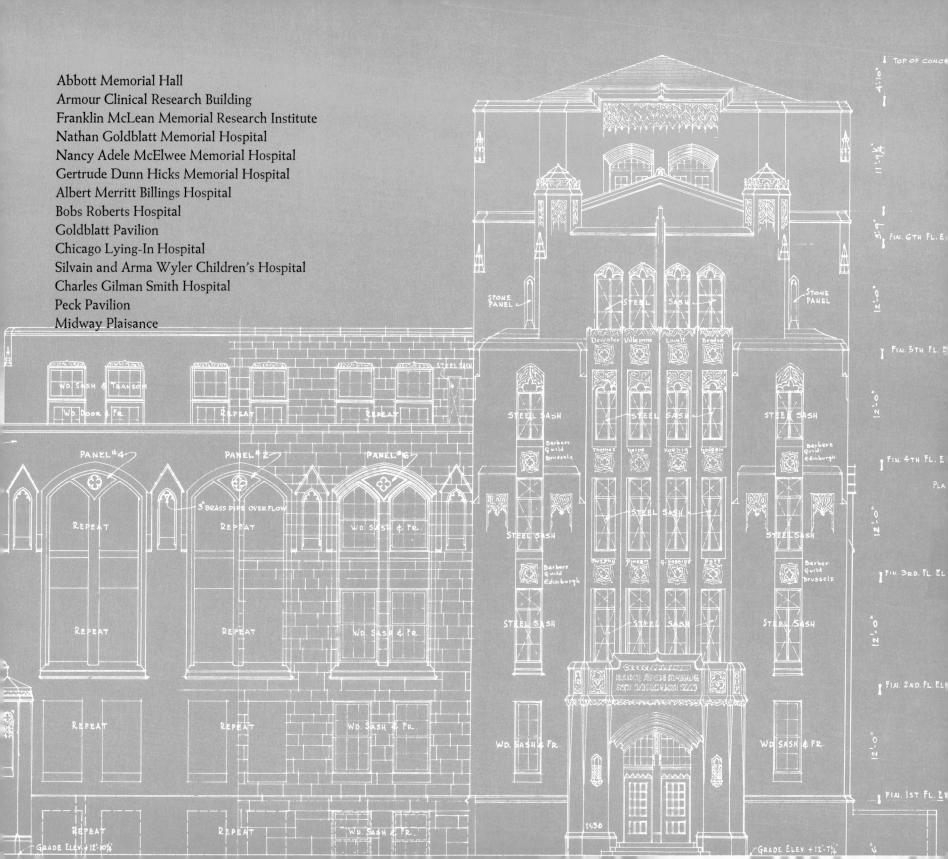

Abbott Memorial Hall
Armour Clinical Research Building
Franklin McLean Memorial Research Institute
Nathan Goldblatt Memorial Hospital
Nancy Adele McElwee Memorial Hospital
Gertrude Dunn Hicks Memorial Hospital
Albert Merritt Billings Hospital
Bobs Roberts Hospital
Goldblatt Pavilion
Chicago Lying-In Hospital
Silvain and Arma Wyler Children's Hospital
Charles Gilman Smith Hospital
Peck Pavilion
Midway Plaisance

Overleaf: Nancy Adele McElwee Memorial Hospital.
Coolidge & Hodgdon, 1931.
South elevation.

Abbott Memorial Hall.

Architects: Coolidge & Hodgdon, 1927.

North entrance archway.

Philip D. Armour Clinical Research Building.
Architects: Schmidt, Garden & Erikson, 1963.

Franklin McLean Memorial Research Institute.
Architects: Schmidt, Garden and Erikson, 1953.

Nathan Goldblatt Memorial Hospital.
Architects: Schmidt, Garden & Erikson, 1950.

Nancy Adele McElwee Memorial Hospital.

Architects: Coolidge & Hodgdon, 1931.

Gertrude Dunn Hicks Memorial Hospital.

Architects: Coolidge & Hodgdon, 1931.

McElwee Memorial Hospital at right.

Albert Merritt Billings Hospital.

Architects: Coolidge & Hodgdon, 1925.

Bobs Roberts Hospital.
Architects: Coolidge & Hodgdon, 1930.

Goldblatt Pavilion.

Architects: Schmidt, Garden & Erikson, 1961.   Out-patient admitting area.

Chicago Lying-in Hospital.
Architects: Schmidt, Garden & Erikson, 1931.

Midway: Looking north and west. Right to left: Harper, Wieboldt, Classics, the Hospitals.

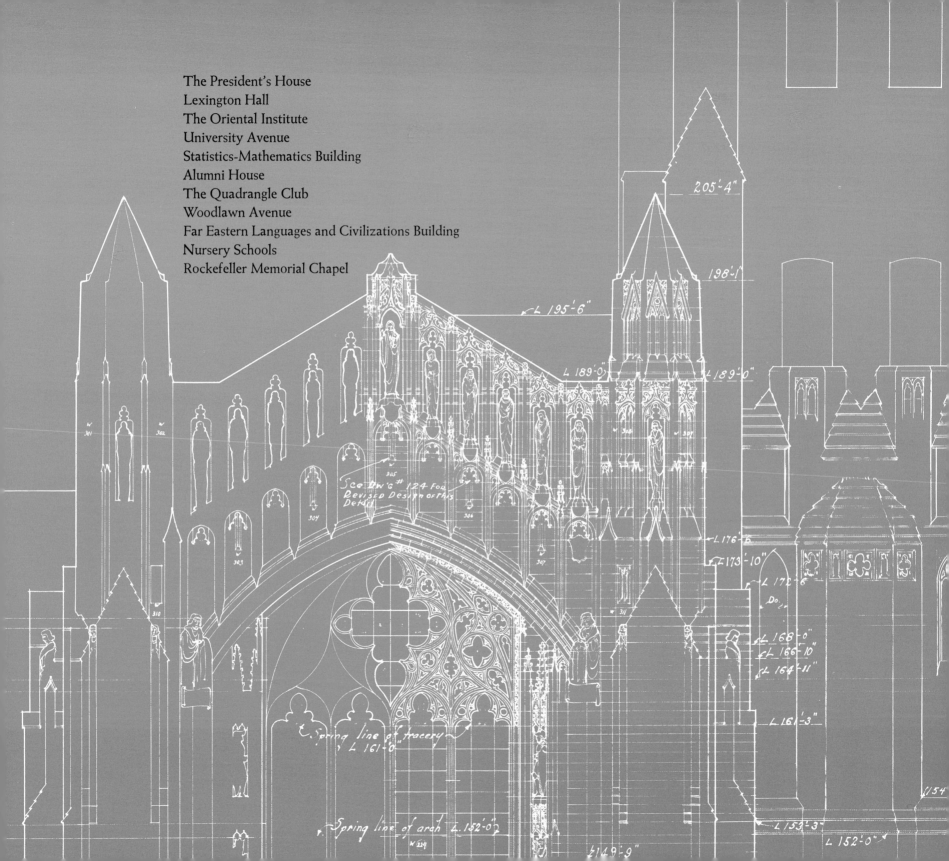

The President's House
Lexington Hall
The Oriental Institute
University Avenue
Statistics-Mathematics Building
Alumni House
The Quadrangle Club
Woodlawn Avenue
Far Eastern Languages and Civilizations Building
Nursery Schools
Rockefeller Memorial Chapel

Overleaf: Rockefeller Memorial Chapel.
Bertram Grosvenor Goodhue, 1925.
South elevation.

The President's House.

Architect: Henry Ives Cobb, 1895.

Renovation of exterior by Coolidge & Hodgdon, 1929; Shaw, Metz & Dolio, 1949.

Renovation of interior by Arthur Myhrum, 1968.

South front, on 59th Street.

173

President's House: Front door and stairwell.

Ground-floor reception room.

Dining room.

First-floor parlor.   Living room.

Lexington Hall.
Architect: James Gamble Rogers, 1903.